Getting Older, Growing Wiser

Getting Older, Growing Wiser

written by
Carol Ann Morrow

illustrated by
R.W. Alley

ONE
CARING
PLACE

Abbey Press

Text © 2000 by Carol Ann Morrow
Illustrations © 2000 by St. Meinrad Archabbey
Published by One Caring Place
Abbey Press
St. Meinrad, Indiana 47577

Library of Congress Catalog Number
00-107871

ISBN 0-87029-349-4

Printed in the United States of America

Foreword

Do you dread birthdays? Do you lie about your age? Are you eligible for benefits and discounts offered to older people—but don't claim them? Are some body parts less dependable than they once were—including your mind and memory?

A poem by Frank Canatella includes this line: "Life is too much to have all at once." Apparently we must take it as it comes—in the order that it's given. You have known a lot of living. Now you face a part of life that many people find daunting and fraught with danger and decline: growing old.

Author Carol Ann Morrow faces aging squarely, showing how to contemplate it with curiosity and expectation. As you journey with her through some of the common dilemmas of growing older, you'll find yourself scaling a mountain range of possibilities—both peaks and pits.

Along the way, you'll find wisdom to help you discover the meaning and mission of your older years—lessons of strength, longevity, and fruitfulness. For, as the esteemed Dr. Seuss says, "You're only old once!"

1.

Every birthday presents a new threshold, an entryway into a place you have never been. If you think of it as the same old place, then you will surely see what you've always seen. Look again—and see something new on the horizon.

2.

You can gather years or you can gather momentum. Keep moving and you will gain power—physical, mental, and emotional.

3.

The passage of years has
piled on many experiences.
The blessing of years is
believing that nothing that
has happened is for nothing.
Harvest the fruits of your years.

4.

It's no accident that this part of life is described as "growing old." You can focus on <u>growing</u> or you can focus on <u>old</u>. <u>Growing</u> is active change and movement. <u>Old</u> is what happens when growing stops.

5.

Bless yourself each morning and ask the Almighty how you can scatter blessings everywhere. How to be a blessing: this is the central question for aging with wisdom and grace.

6.

Resurrect your dreams and pursue them. If the time is past to act on all of them, record them—on paper or on tape. Let your vision inspire another generation.

7.

You can plod or you can play your way through the calendar of advancing years. The first is the heavy weight of obligation. The second is the lightheartedness of a child. Choose your weight class.

CLOWN
CLASS
TODAY ↑

8.

What use is it to have ever
been young, if you cannot
build on that history today?
Recall your youth, not simply
for nostalgia's sake, but to
distill lessons for today.

9.

Your insurance agent may speak of life expectancy. But what your soul requires is expectant life. What do you expect of this day? What can you do to make it happen?

10.

"Maturing" sounds good if you're a savings bond, but it may not seem like such a dividend when you're counting human years. Unless you're ready to cash in, don't mature! Ask questions rather than giving all the answers. Enjoy recess every day. Eat dessert first sometimes!

11.

Get real. Abandon pretense.
Guided by God's inspiration
working within you, learn
who you are and be who
you are. Allow others to
know the real you.

12.

The second half of life is the time to connect your outer self with your inner self, the time to integrate. Be still, let life settle in you. Find your center, where God waits for you.

13.

Attend to your inner life. Ponder the meaning of events— happy and otherwise. You can mine them for their significance or let them go. You can discern which are worth saving and savoring.

14.

When you were younger, you needed excitement to avoid boredom. Age offers the perspective that an ordinary day is brimming with delights. Keep your glasses handy—to notice ordinary wonders.

15.

Expect good to come of each
year ahead, for what we
anticipate often happens.
One advantage of trifocals is
that you can spot the good at
a range of distances—under
your nose or far away.

16.

Love, love, love. You can never grow too old to give and receive love. When you give love, it will come back to rest in your heart, making you whole and spiritually healthy.

17.

Eat wholesome food. Grow
flowers. Read vital books.
Mix with joyous people.
Praise the living God.
Surround yourself with
natural life-support systems!

18.

Give freely of yourself. Dispense and disperse. Contribute your gifts—of time, money, support, goodwill. You can only take it with you if you hold it in an open hand. Then it is credited to your account.

Elf Valley
Food Bank

19.

Sense your connection with all things. You are aging—as is all else that now lives. Respect the wisdom of the earth's cycles of rest and rebirth. Enjoy, participate, and gather energy from the rhythms of nature.

20.

Look to the earth for mentors. You can be an annual blossom that withers after one season in the sun—or a perennial that blooms anew season after season. The flowers don't choose, but you can.

21.

Be curious. Spend some time each day wondering about the world, about your favorite people, about the heavenly mysteries. Look for answers— in books, on the internet, in the experience of others, in prayer. Gather wisdom like a bouquet for your personal delight.

22.

Exercise—whatever moves.
Exercise your arms and legs.
Exercise your mind. Exercise
your senses, your imagination,
your patience, your rights.
Move on.

23.

Appreciate. Let go of
expectations and demands.
Receive everything in life
as gift.

24.

Over the years, life has held many mysteries—some in the stars, others in the heart. You can attend to them now. List what you still don't understand but wish you did. Stretch your mind; expand your spirit to be open to life's wisdom.

25.

Take mental risks—even leaps. Volunteer for a worthy cause. Express your opinion to someone in power. Try a new schedule. Surprise yourself.

26.

Travel enriches the spirit. Even at home, in the view from the window, a sense of exploration and discovery contributes to delight. You can travel far simply by opening your eyes. It's also beneficial to open the door.

27.

Be present. Know where you are—geographically and spiritually. Revel in that time and space today. It's too late to redo yesterday and too early to experience tomorrow.

28.

Age gives you so much more to honor, to treasure. You can lament what is past or you can delight in all the memories— and make new ones by sharing memories and mementos with those not yet blessed by age.

29.

Let go of your rules for others. Allow those who live with you, who love you, who misunderstand you, to be as they are. Give them their freedom and it will free you from any need to manage their lives.

30.

Mend and tend your relationships. Grudges and ill will bend your back, tense your nerves, and tighten your jaw. You can kill yourself clinging to past hurts. You can add years by letting go.

31.

Intend good to everyone you meet—and those beyond your reach. Make efforts to extend goodness into the world through thoughts and acts of kindness. Effort added to intention creates change.

32.

Forgive yourself for your mistakes. Distressed wood is valued for its scars, the evidence of its individuality. You are marked, perhaps scarred as well, but you have survived. Wear your scars as badges of lessons learned and growth earned.

33.

Avoid being housebound—
that is, held fast by your house.
This is most likely to happen
if you've accumulated many
things that require your
attention. Divest yourself
of treasures that own you,
so that you may possess the
treasure of freedom from care.

34.

Make a home within your own heart. Nest there; enjoy the comfort of being at home with yourself. There you will learn to be alone without being lonely.

35.

People you love will die. You
will mourn them and miss
them terribly. But you will
not honor them by dying
before your time. You are
still connected with them
in memory and spirit. Let
this connection inspire and
strengthen you for living.

36.

You may be tested by aches and pains or illness, but you are not your illness. Remember, you are God's creation, challenged by imperfection but with an invincible spirit.

37.

Embrace whatever comes.
Running away saps your energy.
What is held close can be seen
clearly, faced, and befriended.
All will be well.

38.

Every year of your life has been a gift. Every year ahead is also given, not earned. Treat the years as gifts—with daily thanks and reverence. Give yourself to the Giver. Then the final letting go will be but a gentle passage back into God's hands.

Carol Ann Morrow is the author of two other Elf-Help books, *Peace Therapy* and *Trust-in-God Therapy*. Married and living in Cincinnati, she is an associate member of the Oldenburg, Indiana, Sisters of St. Francis, who have taught her a great deal about aging with grace.

Illustrator for the Abbey Press Elf-help Books, **R.W. Alley** also illustrates and writes children's books. He lives in Barrington, Rhode Island, with his wife, daughter, and son.

The Story of the Abbey Press Elves

The engaging figures that populate the Abbey Press "elf-help" line of publications and products first appeared in 1987 on the pages of a small self-help book called *Be-good-to-yourself Therapy*. Shaped by the publishing staff's vision and defined in R.W. Alley's inventive illustrations, they lived out author Cherry Hartman's gentle, self-nurturing advice with charm, poignancy, and humor.

Reader response was so enthusiastic that more Elf-help Books were soon under way, a still-growing series that has inspired a line of related gift products.

The especially endearing character featured in the early books—sporting a cap with a mood-changing candle in its peak—has since been joined by a spirited female elf with flowers in her hair.

These two exuberant, sensitive, resourceful, kindhearted, lovable sprites, along with their lively elfin community, reveal what's truly important as they offer messages of joy and wonder, playfulness and co-creation, wholeness and serenity, the miracle of life and the mystery of God's love.

With wisdom and whimsy, these little creatures with long noses demonstrate the elf-help way to a rich and fulfilling life.

Elf-help Books

...adding "a little character" and a lot
of help to self-help reading!

Book price is $4.95 unless otherwise noted.
Available at your favorite giftshop or bookstore—
or directly from One Caring Place, Abbey Press
Publications, St. Meinrad, IN 47577.
Or call 1-800-325-2511.
www.carenotes.com